ALSO AVAILABLE IN THIS SERIES:
DREAM: The Words and Inspiration of Martin Luther King, Jr.
PEACE: The Words and Inspiration of Mahatma Gandhi
LOVE: The Words and Inspiration of Mother Teresa

Produced and originated by PQ Blackwell Limited
116 Symonds Street, Auckland, New Zealand
www.pqblackwell.com

Distributed exclusively in the United States, Canada, and the Philippines by Blue
Mountain Arts, Inc.

Designed by Cameron Gibb, Annatjie Matthee, and Carolyn Lewis.

Printed by Midas Printing International Ltd., China.

Library of Congress Control Number: 2006909703
ISBN: 978-1-59842-241-2

Acknowledgments appear on page 94.

First Printing: 2007

Blue Mountain Arts, Inc.
P.O. Box 4549, Boulder, Colorado 80306

THE WORDS AND INSPIRATION OF
DESMOND TUTU

INTRODUCTION BY
ARCHBISHOP DESMOND TUTU

Blue Mountain Press®
Boulder, Colorado

"If I diminish you, I diminish myself."

In my culture and tradition the highest praise that can be given to someone is, *"Yu, u nobuntu,"* an acknowledgment that he or she has this wonderful quality, *ubuntu.* It is a reference to their actions toward their fellow human beings. It has to do with how they regard people and how they see themselves within their intimate relationships, their familial relationships, and within the broader community. *Ubuntu* addresses a central tenet of African philosophy, the essence of what it is to be human.

The definition of this concept has two parts. The first is that the person is friendly, hospitable, generous, gentle, caring, and compassionate. In other words, someone who will use his or her strengths on behalf of others — the weak and the poor and the ill — and not take advantage of anyone. This person treats others as he or she would be treated. And because of this they express the second part of the concept, which concerns openness, large-heartedness. They share their worth. In doing so my humanity is recognized and becomes inextricably bound to theirs.

People with *ubuntu* are approachable and welcoming; their attitude is kindly and well-disposed; they are not threatened by the goodness in others because their own esteem and self-worth is generated by knowing they belong to a greater whole. To recast the Cartesian proposition "I think, therefore I am," *ubuntu* would phrase it, "I am human because I belong." Put another way, "a person is a person through other people," a concept perfectly captured by the phrase "me we." No one comes into the world fully formed. We would not know how to think or walk or speak or behave unless we learned it from our fellow human beings. We need other human beings in order to be human. The solitary, isolated human being is a contradiction in terms.

Because we need one another, our natural tendency is to be cooperative and helpful. If this were not true we would have died out as a species long ago, consumed by our violence and hate. But we haven't. We have kept on despite the evil and the wars that have brought so much suffering and misery down the centuries. We have kept on because we strive for harmony and community, a community not only of the living but also one that honors our forebears. This link to the past gives us a sense of continuity; a sense that we have created and create societies that are meant to be for the greater good and try to overcome anything that subverts our purpose. Our wars end; we seek to heal.

But anger, resentment, a lust for revenge, greed, even the aggressive competitiveness that rules so much of our contemporary world, corrodes and jeopardizes our harmony. *Ubuntu* points out that those who seek to destroy and dehumanize are also victims — victims, usually, of a pervading ethos, be it a political ideology, an economic system, or a distorted religious conviction. Consequently, they are as much dehumanized as those on whom they trample.

Never was this more obvious than during the apartheid years in South Africa. All humanity is interlinked. Thus, the humanity of the perpetrators of apartheid was inexorably bound to that of their victims. When they dehumanized another by inflicting suffering and harm, they dehumanized themselves. In fact I said at the time that the oppressor was dehumanized as much as, if not more than, those oppressed. How else could you interpret the words of the minister of police, Jimmy Kruger, on hearing of the death of Black Consciousness leader, Steve Biko, in prison. Of his tortured and painful killing, Kruger said, it "leaves me cold." You have to ask what has happened to the humanity — the *ubuntu* — of someone who could speak so callously about the suffering and death of a fellow human being.

It was equally clear that recovering from this situation would require a magnanimousness on the part of the victims if there was to be a future. The end of apartheid, I knew, would put *ubuntu* to the test. Yet I never doubted its power of reconciliation. In fact I often recalled the words of a man called Malusi Mpumlwana, an associate of Biko's, who, even while he was being tortured by the security police, looked at his torturers and realized that these were human beings too and that they needed him "to help them recover the humanity they [were] losing."

The essence of *ubuntu*, or "me we," could be seen clearly during the Truth and Reconciliation Commission hearings in South Africa in the mid-1990s. Victims forgave their torturers, indeed, even forgave those who, by doing nothing, had supported apartheid. And some perpetrators confessed and asked for forgiveness and were given amnesty. This forgiveness was not about altruism. It was about regaining dignity and humanity and granting these, too, to the former oppressors.

This expression of *ubuntu* showed that the only way we can ever be human is together. The only way we can be free is together.

The Most Reverend Desmond M. Tutu, OMSG DD FKC
Anglican Archbishop Emeritus of Cape Town

Desmond Tutu

Archbishop Desmond Mpilo Tutu

The photograph is black and white. It is taken from low down in a crowd so that the figure of Bishop Desmond Tutu is etched against the sky. He wears the long robes of an Anglican priest; his eyes are shaded by dark glasses. He stands, his arms thrown out like a martyr nailed to an invisible cross.

What the photograph does not show is the harsh white glare of the mid-winter sun or the dust that swirls from beneath the feet of young people as they stamp and shuffle through the *toyi-toyi* war dance. Nor does it show the coffins of fourteen people killed the previous week during political unrest in the South African township of KwaThema outside Johannesburg.

The photograph was taken in July 1985. At the time the country was under a state of emergency as violent uprisings smoldered in the cities and the townships. The previous week in Duduza a woman had been beaten, mutilated, and burnt to death by an angry mob convinced she was an *impimpi*, a betrayer. Hatred and anger were in people's voices and in their eyes.

The funeral service for the fourteen was held in a sports stadium where thirty thousand people had gathered as much to bury the dead as to voice their protest against the draconian apartheid state. When Tutu entered the stadium he was greeted by an ovation that lasted almost fifteen minutes. As it ceased he climbed onto a table and prayed for the dead and the living. He then told the crowd that the killing of the woman the previous week had horrified him as it was an expression of violence enough to make him despair.

"We have a cause that is just," he said. "We have a cause that is going to prevail. For goodness' sake, let us not spoil it by the kind of methods that we use. And if we do this again, I must tell you that I am going to find it difficult to be able to speak up for our liberation. I will find it difficult — it is already difficult in this country to talk the truth — but if we use methods such as the one that we saw in Duduza, then, my friends, I am going to collect my family and leave a country that I love very deeply, a country that I love passionately."[1]

The crowd fell silent. Some booed; most stood with bowed heads while the truth spoken by this man who was their voice at a time when they were voiceless resounded in their hearts.

 The previous month, while he officiated at a funeral, Tutu had been confronted with the very real attempted burning of an *impimpi*. Youths angered by the presence of a policeman had overturned and set fire to the officer's car, beaten him to the ground, and doused him with gasoline. They were about to consign him to the inferno when Tutu and another priest battled through the mêlée to the screaming man. In his long purple cassock and his dark glasses, Tutu could barely be seen above the heads of the youths as he made his way determinedly to the center of the maelstrom. Amidst the shouting and the anger and the heat from the burning car, the bleeding man lay prostrate before him clutching at his ankles. Tutu, on the verge of tears, pleaded with the youths to spare the policeman's life. Reluctantly, they relented and the injured man was bundled into a car and driven off to a hospital. But tempers were raised and not easily pacified; the youths now turned on Tutu.

"Why don't you allow us to deal with these dogs in the same way they treat us?" shouted one, threatening Tutu with a sjambok, a rawhide whip.[2] Undaunted, Tutu responded that he understood their anger and knew that many of them had been betrayed, imprisoned, and killed, but theirs was a noble and righteous struggle and there was no need to resort to the violence of the oppressors. There was no need to kill.

And yet every week there were more funerals as the clashes between activists and heavily armed police and troops intensified. And with every funeral the political temperature rose. Eventually further restrictions were imposed curtailing the size of funerals, preventing marches to the cemeteries, and banning political speeches. A defiant Tutu ignored the new rulings. At the funeral of three teenage boys shot dead by police he told more than ten thousand mourners: "I will not listen to people who tell me what to preach… I will preach the Gospel of Jesus Christ… If they pass laws which are quite unjust, quite intolerable, then I will break the law."[3]

Five days later at the funeral of a young girl, he did. Police and soldiers in armored vehicles lined the route to the cemetery and ordered a small crowd of about fifteen hundred to disperse. The people became militant. Tutu stepped between the armed forces who clutched automatic rifles and the mourners armed with stones and sticks, and said, "Please allow us to bury our dead with dignity. Please do not rub our noses in the dust. We are already hurt, we are already down. Don't trample on us. We are human beings, we are not animals. And when we have a death, we cry like you cry."[4] After twenty minutes of negotiation with the police, he convinced them that the funeral should proceed.

But while Tutu was venerated in the townships, whenever he tried to suppress the violence, he personally walked ever closer to the dangerous edge of a people driven to desperation. In Alexandra township, Johannesburg, he pleaded with a crowd of forty thousand gathered in a football stadium not to confront the security forces. For years the township had suffered a heavy police presence; for months the confrontations between the police and the residents had escalated — always there were deaths. Tutu intervened by promising to approach state president P. W. Botha, but in the end the president refused to see him. Tutu returned to Alexandra with nothing to offer: no hope, no concessions. The crowed rebelled, booed him, shouted at him that the deaths had to be avenged. As he left the stadium youths surrounded him, taunting him with what they would do when he was gone.

But although the violence would continue and worsen over the next eight years until the first democratic election of 1994, and although Tutu would literally shed tears at the anguish of a nation in torment, he did not abandon his congregation. Whenever he needed to step into the frontline he would. Nor did he abandon his crusade for nonviolence. Killing was wrong. He abhorred the bloodshed.

The life of Archbishop Desmond Tutu has been defined by politics and history. In another time and in another place he may have been no more remarkable than a much loved pastor of the people. But his time dictated otherwise. And he responded as a moral light that challenged not only the darkness created by the state but the darkness that enveloped his people. He was their voice and their conscience — as well as the conscience of those who oppressed them. When he was called to face the armor and the weaponry of government, he knelt on the pavement before the security forces and prayed — prayers that were offered as much for one side as the other.

Desmond Mpilo Tutu was born on October 7, 1931 in the small town of Klerksdorp, some hundred and thirty kilometers to the west of Johannesburg. In his first ten years he would move homes four times as his father and mother sought to provide for their family during a difficult decade. He also was beset by disease and accident. If his life is characterized by a pattern, it is of movement and change, of having to adapt to ever fluid circumstances.

Tutu was born of "rainbow" parents — to use a metaphor he would apply many decades later to the nation. His father was a Xhosa-speaker, his mother a Motswana from a different language group and culture. According to patriarchal custom, the family spoke the father's language and followed Xhosa traditions. Tutu was the couple's third child — the first, a son, had died in infancy, and he himself seemed destined for the same fate. Sickly from birth, within his first year he contracted polio, a disease then with a mortality rate of 25 percent. His father, convinced the baby boy would die, prepared a funeral, but against the odds Tutu recovered, although his right hand had atrophied. (Over the years he developed a habit of rubbing this hand to improve the circulation. In the political turbulence of the 1980s, the gesture would be interpreted by his detractors as evidence of a troublesome priest's guilt and duplicity.) The young Tutu had no sooner recovered from the polio than he had to be hospitalized with serious burns to his thigh. On an icy winter morning he stood too close to an outdoor brazier and his pajamas caught fire.

As if these traumas were not enough, his father's occupation as a schoolteacher took him from one school to another, and the family had to move again. Then, because his income proved insufficient, Tutu's mother was forced to seek domestic work in distant Johannesburg to supplement the family's finances. Eventually, when Tutu began his high school years, the family was reunited in the township of Munsieville. For some of the time prior, Tutu lived in a hostel in Sopiatown near his mother. He greatly admired her: found her gentle, compassionate and caring, always ready to take the side of the underdog, always prepared to share — qualities which would manifest time and again in his own life. Once, on a cold railway station as he waited for the early morning train to school, he noticed a boy shivering in the cutting wind. Quickly, he took off one of the two jerseys he wore and gave it to the boy, begging his sister not to tell their mother.

The young Tutu, while occupied with his own world, was increasingly becoming aware of a racial divide. White people had better houses, better schools. Their children often threw away their lunch sandwiches half eaten, which he found strange but initially did not question — as he did not question the hunger that drove his friends to scavenge these remains from the trash bins. Yet when a shopkeeper called his father "boy," Tutu bristled at the insult, just as he marvelled when a white priest greeted his mother by doffing his hat. White people did not treat black people with any respect, and this fact deeply affected the future archbishop.

Tutu's high school years were spent at the progressive, well respected if robust Western High near the bohemian Johannesburg suburb of Sophiatown. Ten years later, in the mid-1950s, the community would be forcibly removed to various townships and the area occupied by whites and renamed Triomf (triumph). In the meantime it provided a culturally rich and uncharacteristically nonracial background to his schooling. Two years into his time at Western High, fourteen-year-old Tutu contracted tuberculosis. For the next twenty months he was confined to a state-run sanatorium. Yet not even this depressing institution could quell Tutu's inherent optimism. When his friends visited he wanted to know what they had learned in school. When they brought him comics he asked for novels instead.

It was during these months that he began a friendship with Father Trevor Huddleston, the legendary priest of Sophiatown who would try to intercede on his parishioners' behalf when the removals started. Huddleston greatly influenced Tutu's religious direction, for although the Tutu family were devout worshippers, their adherence was more to the central concepts of Christianity than to any denomination, although Tutu was baptized a Methodist. Tutu left the sanatorium with a sense of the spiritual, which was to intensify over the years, and a leaning toward the Anglican Church. He became more involved in the local parish church and would often slip off to pray, occasionally for as long as an hour.

Yet when he matriculated, Tutu's thoughts were toward practicing medicine rather than the ministry. As it happened he did neither, becoming like his father before him a teacher, one who inspired his classes with his energy, sense of humor, and enthusiasm for living. Discipline was never a problem; his pupils adored him because he treated them gently and humanely — two attributes that would resonate throughout his life. Thus, even in the junior teacher could be seen the attitude of the future prelate and leader who would face the most dangerous of standoffs with a quiet courage that was sure to defuse the situation.

The school where Tutu taught was situated in a rough part of the township. *Tsotsis* — gangsters — ruled the streets with knives and guns. When a group of thugs came to the school literally hunting for girls, the headmaster, the teachers, and the pupils panicked, barricading themselves in the classrooms. Tutu, however, would have none of it. He went out to reproach the gangsters. Soon he was joking with them, and as the tension evaporated the thugs put away their guns and sauntered off. It was the first of many such incidents in the life of Desmond Tutu.

Tutu's teaching career came to an end with the implementation of the Bantu Education Act in 1955 by the apartheid government. The tenor and practice of this act was to downgrade the syllabus for black school children in preparation for a life of manual — and menial — labor. Tutu, who valued education and knowledge as a means toward freedom and independence, could not be party to such a system. He and Leah, his schoolteacher wife of a year, resigned their posts.

Tutu's thoughts now turned toward the ministry. However, it was a consideration not taken lightly. His father, some of his friends, and even some of his pupils felt that he was wasting his talents, but the man himself was convinced. He later referred to his decision as "God grabbing me by the scruff of my neck."[5] By 1960 Tutu had completed his studies and was ordained a deacon. By the following year he became a priest. Nothing delighted him more in his new duties than visiting his parishioners: taking communion to the sick and the aged, dropping in on the lonely and the destitute. "You can't love people and not visit them," he told a biographer. "You can't love them unless you know them, and you can't know them unless you visit them regularly. A good shepherd knows his sheep by name."[6]

But once again the life of the ardent pastor was disrupted when he was invited to study for a bachelor of divinity at King's College, London. Tutu would end up spending the next five years in England completing two degrees: a bachelor's and a master's. He also worked as a curate throughout his stay, finishing his last eleven months in the parish of Bletchingley, a community of "landed gentry" and farm workers. To all of them, black skin was a rarity. But Tutu brought to the parish such wit and vitality that the villagers took him and his family into their hearts. If his years in England freed him from the yoke of apartheid, they also showed him how that yoke could oppress: "The most horrible aspect of apartheid, a blasphemous aspect, is it can make a child of God doubt that they are a child of God, when you ask yourself in the middle of the night, 'God, am I your step-child?'"[7]

The time of freedom ended and reluctantly the family returned to South Africa, Tutu taking up a teaching position at the Theological Seminary at Alice in the Eastern Cape. He was also chaplain of the nearby University of Fort Hare, the academic alma mater of so many of the country's political leaders, including Nelson Mandela. And it was here that Tutu for the first time stepped onto the political battlefield. By then, late in 1968, a new movement known as black consciousness — a call for black people to realize their self-worth — was rekindling opposition to apartheid. After the Sharpeville massacre of 1960, where police shot dead at least sixty-nine people, and the capture and incarceration on Robben Island of many of the black leaders, opposition had been silenced. But now the first stirrings of renewed resistance were being heard, particularly at the University of Fort Hare. When police in armored cars arrived on campus to suppress a demonstration, Tutu hurried over from the seminary to ensure there were no arrests or violent incidents. The police tried to stop him, but he thrust through their ranks to side with the students. "If you are arresting the students you can count me as their chaplain with them," he retorted.[8]

The encounter shifted something deep inside Tutu. His experience among white people in England led him to believe that if the conscience of white people in South Africa could be awakened to the hurt of apartheid, then nonracial cooperation would lead to a change in the country's politics. But the brutality of the police depressed him. He questioned his God. The next day at Mass he broke down and cried. He identified strongly with the students and with the principles of black consciousness, yet, at a point when he was beginning to internalize the struggle against oppression, again the pattern of his life intervened to end his tenure at the seminary in 1969.

For the next four years Tutu lived outside South Africa, first in Lesotho teaching theology at the University of Botswana, then in London serving as an associate director at the World Council of Churches. This position gave him access to many countries and he traveled widely, particularly in Africa. The experience alerted him to disparities between church and state throughout the African continent — even in those states recently liberated from colonialism — and helped him refine his theological thinking. In a paper he wrote: "Black theology has to do with whether it is possible to be black and continue to be Christian; it is to ask on whose side is God; it is to be concerned about the humanization of man, because those who ravage our humanity dehumanize themselves in the process; [it says] that the liberation of the black man is the other side of the coin of the liberation of the white man — so it is concerned with human liberation."[9] This became a guiding note in everything Tutu was to do upon his return to South Africa in 1975. From then through to the hearings of that country's Truth and Reconciliation Commission thirty years later, these ideas were fundamental to Tutu's attitude toward humanity. And most notable is his formulation of the *ubuntu* idiom: "A person is a person through other people."

Tutu's return to South Africa was nothing if not controversial. While still in London he had been nominated as a candidate for the position of Bishop of Johannesburg and had narrowly been defeated in the election. However, the new bishop, keen to alter the church's white hierarchy, appointed him head of St. Mary's Cathedral in Johannesburg, the first black cleric to hold the position. The appointment pushed Tutu willy-nilly onto the public stage. Until this point, his had not been a political voice, and his rise in the church had been determined by his intellect, wit, and buoyant personality. Now his role as pastor extended beyond administering to his congregation. In his first weeks as dean he shared a platform with Winnie Mandela and explained the theological reasons for opposing such harsh legislation as the Terrorism Act. He held a twenty-four hour prayer vigil for those detained without trial under the act, and he began to petition the state and white society. His message was simple: the country teetered close to a political explosion.

In May 1976, he warned in an article published in a Johannesburg newspaper about a pending "bloody confrontation."[10] A few days later while on a retreat, he felt called on by God to write to the prime minister, John Vorster. He did so, appealing to the man's humanity, to his religious convictions, to his feelings as a father and grandfather, concluding with the portentous words: "I am frightened, dreadfully frightened, that we may soon reach a point of no return, when events will generate a momentum of their own, when nothing will stop their reaching a bloody denouement…"[11] Six weeks later the "explosion" came when black school children in Soweto rebelled against the education system and sparked a series of violent uprisings which engulfed the country. Tutu responded by holding prayer vigils, by being constantly visible in the townships, and by exhorting his white congregants to condemn the suppression. Their lack of compassion profoundly disturbed him.

Then Tutu's life took another unexpected turn: he was elected Bishop of Lesotho. Suddenly, in the midst of ministering to the urgent needs of his homeland, he was being whisked away again. And while he had long wanted to be a bishop, the circumstances seemed inappropriate. However, as in all things, he put his heart into his congregation in the tiny mountain kingdom, even while he watched his beloved country becoming increasingly volatile. And then, in the roller coaster pattern of Tutu's life, two years later he again faced a career crisis when he was approached by the South African Council of

Churches to become the general secretary. The position was highly influential, and the six years that Tutu occupied it became known as "the hottest ecclesiastical seat in the country."[12]

Although he was without a parish, Tutu felt compelled to speak out about the increasing polarization between the church and the state. While remaining ardently pacifist, he said he understood why young black people resorted to arms. He argued for economic sanctions and boycotts against the country and South African businesses and for the disinvestment of multinationals. He acknowledged that in the short term this might lead to job losses and increase the suffering of black people, but it would hasten the end of apartheid. If these were the statements of a political priest, he remained, too, a pastor, concerned for the welfare of his people. And the places he hurried to were the sites of forced removals and the dumping grounds of the Bantustans.

In the drive to create a white South Africa and a host of black puppet states, the apartheid government forcibly removed whole villages within "white areas" and resettled them in the Bantustans, often on barren land. Tutu made a point of visiting these places and praying with the people. For years the words of a hungry little girl he encountered on one of these dumping grounds haunted him and haunted his letters, begging compassion from the new prime minister and latter-day state president, P. W. Botha. When asked what she did when she was hungry and no one had food to spare, the little girl said, "We drink water to fill our stomachs."[13] Tutu was overcome with pity.

Across South Africa, his actions and statements made him increasingly unpopular among whites. Right-wing Anglicans called on church leaders to censure him. Almost every time he spoke he risked prosecution or banning under the security laws. Inevitably, he was arrested during a highly public march in support of a colleague detained by the police. The march was brought to a halt outside the offices of *The Star* newspaper by a squad of heavily armed riot police wearing camouflage uniforms. The entire leadership was arrested and locked up in the cells at the notorious John Vorster Square police station. Uncowed, Tutu led his colleagues in prayer and the singing of hymns. The following day, all were fined under the Riotous Assemblies Act and released.

Throughout the 1980s, Tutu became a major figure in the struggle against apartheid. He visited political detainees and their families, he officiated at funerals, he led marches, and he held prayer vigils. In the midst of escalating state and mob violence, he spoke out against the bloodlust, including the barbaric practice of "necklacing" people accused of betrayal by setting them afire with gasoline-soaked tires around their necks. Being the voice of the voiceless was not a position Tutu relished or wanted: he was not a political priest, rather a priest driven to politics. But like a prophet he wore the mantle and spoke his mind. For this he aroused great hatred and anger, which resulted in his receiving death threats, hate mail, and obscene telephone calls.

From 1984, Tutu's life became increasingly frenzied. That year he had received a number of honors from institutions and universities in the United States and United Kingdom and, from Oslo, the prestigious Nobel Peace Prize. Yet even before he could attend the Nobel ceremony, his status changed as he was elected Bishop of Johannesburg, the first black priest to hold this position. In Oslo, ever conscious that the award was as much for those he represented as himself, Tutu heard the chairman of the Nobel Committee recount seeing televised footage of a massacre where Tutu "stood and spoke to a frightened and bitter congregation," urging them, "Do not hate, let us choose the peaceful way to freedom."[14] It was a message the bishop continued preaching back home, even while the number of fatalities rose.

In 1986, the speed of events again disrupted Tutu's life when he was elected Archbishop of Cape Town, becoming the head of the Anglican Church in the country — again the first black person to occupy the position. With characteristic impish delight he told reporters: "I'm tongue-tied, and some people hope it's permanent."[15]

If there was an image of Tutu that typified him in his new role as archbishop ("Call me Arch" was an injunction he had printed on T-shirts), it was a march he led through the streets of Cape Town in September 1989. A series of marches and demonstrations at churches in the city had preceded this climax, including a tense occasion in the township of Gugulethu. Here, children and teachers were threatening to march on the local police station to demand the release of detainees. Oily black smoke rose from burning barricades. Tutu, fearing the police would retaliate with violence, intervened and persuaded the demonstrators to disperse. But for his pains, as he and his cohorts left, the security forces fired tear-gas at them.

The mood that month was fraught; the death toll in Cape Town for the first few weeks of September climbed into the twenties. A week later, Tutu's wife was arrested for a few hours for attempting to deliver a petition to the British embassy calling on Margaret Thatcher to apply sanctions. And then, convinced that God had called on him to head a march for peace, Tutu organized and led thirty thousand people — from shop assistants to unionists to white schoolchildren in their uniforms — on a peaceful procession that stretched for two kilometers through the city. Office workers leaned from their windows and cheered, traffic came to a standstill, the marchers sang and *toyi-toyied*.

At the city hall Tutu asked the crowd to hold hands and exhorted the government: "Come and see what this country is going to become. This country is a rainbow country! This country is technicolor! You can come and see the new South Africa!"[16] That march broke the government's ban on protest marches. It also heralded the beginning of a new era as the liberation movements were unbanned and political leaders released from prison. Change was in the air, and talks toward a negotiated settlement started. Even so, violence continued to wrack the country and Tutu continued to visit sites of massacres, to pray at funerals, and to head religious delegations on missions to keep the fragile peace negotiations on track.

After the inauguration of the new government in 1994, Tutu hoped that his days as a political pastor had ended, but he was soon to be called on to head the country's Truth and Reconciliation Commission. The idea behind the commission, one which Tutu championed, was for victims to have a forum where they could tell their stories. It also gave perpetrators of atrocities an opportunity to confess and, under certain circumstances, be granted amnesty. Tutu was a natural choice for the position of chairman. No one else had the moral authority or the compassion and empathy, let alone the sense of humor, needed to guide such an emotional process.

Although he assumed the role of facilitator and conciliator readily, the experience took its emotional toll. While listening to the testimony of an elderly torture victim, Tutu bent face-down onto the table and wept. Proceedings were adjourned, but even after they resumed Tutu had to bite his lip or a finger whenever his emotions welled up. Similarly, at the end of an amnesty hearing for former state president, F.W. de Klerk, Tutu was found by a journalist slumped in his chair, his shoulders rounded in defeat. Why, Tutu wondered, could the man not make an unconditional apology for the suffering his policies had caused? For Tutu, steeped in the traditions of *ubuntu*, such deliberate callousness meant de Klerk was denying his own humanity. Tutu felt devastated and close to tears.

To many, Tutu was the truth commission: his response was the response of the nation. It was even believed by many that without Tutu there could have been no truth commission and that he was vital to its performance. At the end of the proceedings Alex Boraine, the deputy chairman, commented: "I don't think the commission could have survived without the presence and person and leadership of Desmond Tutu."[17]

At the end of the hearings, Tutu, now retired from the archbishopric, might have believed that finally he was due a quiet life of prayer and contemplation. But despite personal health concerns that resulted in a number of operations for prostate cancer, he continued to speak out about injustice, greed, and violence wherever it might loom in the world. And at home he remained a moral force, chastising the new government when he detected corruption and avarice or a failure to address the needs of the citizenry. Once, many years before at an All Africa Conference of Churches, he had told the assembly: "We are true witnesses if we are on the side of the weak, the powerless, the exploited."[18] His attitude was as clear as it had ever been, his ardor undiminished.

Mike Nicol
Cape Town, 2006

A time of crisis is not just a time of anxiety and worry. It gives a chance, an opportunity, to choose well or to choose badly.

This is a moral universe, which means that despite all the evidence that seems to be to the contrary, there is no way that evil and injustice and oppression and lies can have the last word... that is what has upheld the morale of our people, to know that in the end good will prevail.

In a situation where human life seems dirt cheap, with people being killed as easily as one swats a fly, we must proclaim that people matter and matter enormously.

If we have loved
well while we were
alive, there is life
after death here —
our love will go on
for generations.

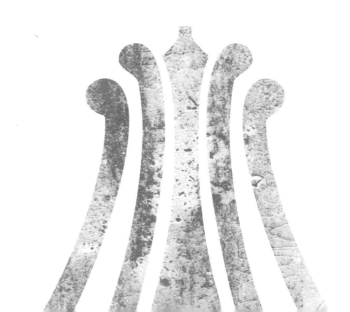

I'm coming to believe more and more in the truth that everything we do has consequences. A good deed doesn't just evaporate and disappear.

TO FORGIVE IS NOT JUST TO BE ALTRUISTIC.

A person is a person

through other persons.

None of us comes into the world fully formed. We would not know how to think, or walk, or speak, or behave as human beings unless we learned it from other human beings. We need other human beings in order to be human. I am because other people are.

A person is entitled to a stable community life, and the first of these communities is the family.

In a happy family you don't receive in proportion to your input. You receive in relation to your needs.

If we could but recognize our common humanity, that we do belong together, that our destinies are bound up in one another's, that we can be free only together, that we can survive only together, that we can be human only together, then a glorious world would come into being where all of us lived harmoniously together as members of one family, the human family.

WE CAN BE HUMAN ONLY TOGETHER.

Children are a wonderful gift. They are young and small persons with minds and ideas, hating to be talked down to. They have an extraordinary capacity to see into the heart of things and to expose sham and humbug for what they are.

Children learn about the nature of the world from their family. They learn about power and about justice, about peace and about compassion within the family. Whether we oppress or liberate our children in our relationships with them will determine whether they grow up to oppress and be oppressed or to liberate and be liberated.

My father always used to say, "Don't raise your voice. Improve your argument." Good sense does not always lie with the loudest shouters, nor can we say that a large, unruly crowd is always the best arbiter of what is right.

I have heard and seen many examples of the cruelty
that we are able to visit on one another during my
time… I have also seen incredible forgiveness and
compassion… Yes, each of us has the capacity for
great evil… But for every act of evil there are a dozen
acts of goodness in our world that go unnoticed... It is
only because we believe that people should be good
that we despair when they are not. Indeed, if people
condoned the evil, we would be justified in losing
hope. But most of the world does not. We know that
we are meant for better.

I LOVE TO BE LOVED.

Freedom is so much a part of the human makeup that it is not too far-fetched to say that an un-free human being is in a sense a contradiction in terms. The ideal society is one in which its members enjoy their freedom to be human freely, provided they do not thereby infringe the freedom of others unduly. We are made to have freedom of association, of expression, of movement, the freedom to choose who will rule over us and how. We are made for this. It is ineluctable. It cannot ultimately be eradicated, this yearning for freedom to be human. This is what tyrants and unjust rulers have to contend with. They cannot in the end stop their victims from being human. Their unjust regimes must ultimately fall because they seek to deny something that cannot be denied.

Just show me your hands, what are you carrying in your hands? Show me! Show me, show me… Your hands are empty, you've got nothing! Why are they so scared of empty hands?... It is important for you to know that all moral right is on your side. Yes, you may be clobbered, as some of you have been clobbered, yes, you may cry, you may get beaten… Some are still going to be detained. Some are still going to run the gauntlet of tear gas. Some are even going to die. Did you think it was figures of speech? When we said that in a struggle there are casualties, did you think it was figures of speech? It is not figures of speech. This is for real, this is real. And we have committed ourselves, we have committed ourselves to this struggle until freedom is won. But we shouldn't behave like those who think this prize is just a cheap little prize. The prize for which we are striving is freedom, is freedom for all of us, freedom for those people standing outside [the police], freedom for them! Because, you see, when we are free, when we are free, they will be here, they will be here, joining with us celebrating that freedom, and not standing outside there stopping us from becoming free... Now straighten up your shoulders, come, straighten up your shoulders like people who are born for freedom!

{ Extract from an address to shocked marchers who had escaped arrest at St. George's Cathedral after being surrounded by police and beaten with batons and whips. Over two hundred other marchers had been arrested. Tutu negotiated with police for the peaceful dispersion of the congregation, September

1989 }

EQUALITY IS ESSENTIAL TO HUMAN LIFE AND WELL-BEING.

Differences are not intended to separate, to alienate. We are different precisely in order to realize our need of one another.

I cannot be opposed to racism, in which people are discriminated against as a result of something about which they can do nothing — their skin color — and then accept with equanimity the gross injustice of penalizing others for something else they can do nothing about — their gender.

There is an old film called *The Defiant Ones*. In one scene, two convicts manacled together escape. They fall into a ditch with slippery sides. One of them claws his way to near the top and just about makes it. But he cannot. His mate to whom he is manacled is still at the bottom and drags him down. The only way they can escape to freedom is together. The one convict was black and the other white: a dramatic parable of our situation in South Africa. The only way we can survive is together, black and white; the only way we can be truly human is together, black and white.

54

Our worth is intrinsic to who we are, depending on nothing extrinsic, whether it be achievement, race, gender, or whatever else.

What does the color of one's skin tell us that is of any significance about a person? Nothing, of course, absolutely nothing. It does not say whether the person is warmhearted or kind, clever and witty, or whether that person is good.

When you have a hand and you have only the separate fingers, it is easy for people to break the fingers. But when you put the fingers together it is difficult to break them. Let us come together and be one, let us be people of peace, let us be people of harmony.

{ Extract from an address to mourners at a mass funeral in Jabulani Stadium, Soweto, August

1990 }

Those who forget the past, as many have pointed out, are doomed to repeat it.

One has got to say to our people, "I love you, I care for you, enormously." And when I care about black liberation, it is because I care about white liberation.

NOTHING IS TOO MUCH TROUBLE FOR LOVE.

We get most upset with those we love the most because they are close to us and we know that they are aware of our weaknesses… If only we could learn to live with our inadequacies, our frailties, our vulnerabilities, we would not need to try so hard to push away those who really know us.

We can love others with their failures when we stop despising ourselves because of our failures.

Many people ask me what I have learned from all of the experiences in my life, and I say unhesitatingly: People are wonderful. It is true. People really *are* wonderful.

PEACE WITHOUT JUSTICE IS AN IMPOSSIBILITY.

To be neutral in a situation of injustice is to have chosen sides already. It is to support the status quo.

Peace involves inevitable righteousness, justice, wholesomeness, fullness of life, participation in decision making, goodness, laughter, joy, compassion, sharing, and reconciliation.

When we look squarely at injustice and get involved, we actually feel less pain, not more, because we overcome the gnawing guilt and despair that festers under our numbness. We clean the wound — our own and others' — and it can finally heal.

All of us experience fear, but when we confront and acknowledge it, we are able to turn it into courage. Being courageous does not mean never being scared; it means acting as you know you must even though you are undeniably afraid.

We humans can tolerate suffering

but we cannot tolerate meaninglessness.

At times of despair, we must learn to
see with new eyes.

Inequality in death results from our
separating ourselves from one another
in life. In war, for example, we keep
score of our casualties to see who is
winning… We become unable to see
their dead as we mourn our own…
Perhaps only when we care about each
other's dead can we truly learn to live
in the same world together without our
irrational prejudices and hatreds.

Have you seen a symphony orchestra?... There is a chap at the back carrying a triangle. Now and again the conductor will point to him and he will play "ting." That might seem so insignificant, but in the conception of the composer something irreplaceable would be lost to the total beauty of the symphony if that "ting" did not happen.

{ Extract from a sermon at University of Natal, Durban, August

1981 }

Forgiveness gives us the capacity to make a new start... And forgiveness is the grace by which you enable the other person to get up, and get up with dignity, to begin anew... In the act of forgiveness we are declaring our faith in the future of a relationship and in the capacity of the wrongdoer to change.

For true reconciliation is a deeply personal matter. It can happen only between persons who assert their own personhood and who acknowledge and respect that of others.

{ Extract from a speech given at Steve Biko's funeral, September

1977}

Utter only the words of which we won't be ashamed afterwards, which we won't regret saying. It is easy to discourage, it is far too easy, all too easy to criticize, to complain, to rebuke. Let us try instead to be more quick to see even a small amount of good in a person and concentrate on that. Let us be more quick to praise than to find fault. Let us be more quick to thank others than to complain — "thank you" and "please" are small words, but they are oh, so powerful.

We should be generous in our judgments of others, for we can never really know all there is to know about another.

Sometimes our technological expertise has seemed to top our moral capacity to use this expertise for the good of humanity. We have a capacity to feed all and yet millions starve because we seem to lack the moral and political will to do what we know is right.

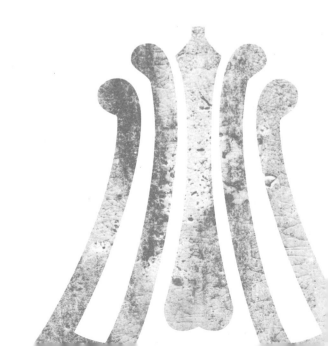

Harmony, friendliness, community are great goods. Social harmony is for us the *summmum bonum* — the greatest good. Anything that subverts, that undermines this sought-after good, is to be avoided like the plague. Anger, resentment, lust for revenge, even success through aggressive competitiveness, are corrosive of this good.

We have tended to treat the weak, the
poor, the unemployed, the failures with
disdain because success and power have
become the gods at whose altars we have
burned incense and bowed the knee.
We have tended to be embarrassed by
compassion and caring as things that
were inappropriate in the harsh, callous
world of business.

It is unity we are talking about, not uniformity. What is needed is to respect one another's points of view and not to impute unworthy motives to one another or to seek to impugn the integrity of the other. Our maturity will be judged by how well we are able to agree to disagree and yet continue to love one another and to cherish one another and seek the greater good of the other.

{ Extract from Archbishop Tutu's archiepiscopacy sermon during his enthronement in St. George's Cathedral as the first black Archbishop of Cape Town, September

1986 }

To ignore people of other faiths and ideologies in an increasingly plural society is to be willfully blind... We are severely impoverished if we do not encounter people of other faiths with reverence and respect for their belief and integrity.

Arrogance really comes from insecurity, and in the end our feeling that we are bigger than others is really the flip side of our feeling that we are smaller than others.

Instead of separation and division, all distinctions make for a rich diversity to be celebrated for the sake of the unity that underlies them. We are different so that we can know our need of one another.

CHARITY

A royalty from the sale of this book will be donated by Archbishop Desmond Tutu to the Tygerberg Children's Hospital and Philani Clinic.

ACKNOWLEDGMENTS

The publisher is grateful for permissions to reproduce material subject to copyright. Every effort has been made to trace the copyright holders and the publisher apologizes for any unintentional omission. We would be pleased to hear from any not acknowledged here and undertake to make all reasonable efforts to include the appropriate acknowledgment in any subsequent editions.

Extracts from *Rabble Rouser for Peace — The Authorized Biography of Desmond Tutu* by John Allen, copyright © 2006 John Allen, reprinted with permission of The Free Press, a Division of Simon & Schuster Adult Publishing Group (North America); and published by Rider and reprinted with permission of The Random House Group Ltd (UK/Commonwealth). All rights reserved. Extracts from *God Has a Dream — A Vision of Hope for Our Time* by Desmond Tutu and Douglas Abrams, copyright © 2004 Desmond Tutu, and *No Future Without Forgiveness* by Desmond Tutu, copyright © 1999 Desmond Tutu, reprinted with permission of Doubleday, a division of Random House Inc. (North America); and published by Rider and reprinted with permission of The Random House Group Ltd (UK/Commonwealth). Extracts from *The Rainbow People of God* by Desmond Tutu and John Allen, editor, copyright © 1994 Desmond Tutu and John Allen, reprinted with permission of Doubleday, a division of Random House Inc. (North America). Extracts from *Tutu — Voice of the Voiceless* by Shirley Du Boulay, reprinted with permission of David Higham Associates. All rights reserved. All other quotations by Desmond Tutu copyright © Desmond M. Tutu. Used with permission. Extract from Nobel Prize speech by Egil Aarvik copyright © The Nobel Foundation 1984. Images used with permission of the following copyright holders: p. 2 © Matt Hoyle; pp. 6, 12, 18, 27, 56 and 86 © Getty Images; pp. 41, 70–71 and 78 © AFP/Getty Images; p. 21 (also cover) © PANAPRESS/Getty Images; p. 9 © William Campbell/Sygma/CORBIS; p. 17 © David Turnley/CORBIS.

The publisher would like to thank the following people.

Archbishop Tutu for his generous support of the Ubuntu Collection; and Lynn Franklin, Archbishop Tutu's literary agent, for her kind assistance with the series and with this book in particular.

Mike Nicol for his insightful biographical essay. Mike Nicol has had a distinguished career both in South Africa and in the UK as an author, journalist and poet. He is the author of four critically acclaimed novels published in South Africa, the U.S., the UK, France and Germany. His best-known nonfiction work is his book on *Drum* magazine, *A Good-Looking Corpse* (Secker & Warburg, 1991), widely regarded as one of the most compelling accounts of the vibrant culture in the black townships of the 1950s.

Thanks also to Jenny Clements for text research and Simon Elder for picture research.

SELECT BIBLIOGRAPHY

Allen, John, *Rabble Rouser for Peace — The Authorized Biography of Desmond Tutu* (Free Press, New York, 2006).
Du Boulay, Shirley, *Tutu — Voice of the Voiceless* (Hodder & Stoughton, London, 1988).
Tutu, Desmond, *No Future Without Forgiveness* (Doubleday, New York, 1999).
— *God Has a Dream — A Vision of Hope for Our Time* (Doubleday, New York, 2004).
— and Mutloatse, Mothobi and Webster, John (eds.), *Hope and Suffering — Sermons and Speeches* (Skotaville Publishers, Johannesburg, 1984).
— and Allen, John (ed.), *The Rainbow People of God* (Doubleday, New York, 1994)
Tutu, Naomi, *The Words of Desmond Tutu* (Newmarket Press, New York, 1989).

NOTES FOR THE BIBLIOGRAPHIC ESSAY

1 Allen, John, *Rabble Rouser for Peace — The Authorized Biography of Desmond Tutu*, 226; 2 Ibid. 225; 3 Ibid. 228; 4 Ibid. 228; 5 Du Boulay, Shirley, *Tutu — Voice of the Voiceless*, 46; 6 Ibid. 56; 7 Ibid. 58; 8 Ibid. 79; 9 Allen, John, *Rabble Rouser for Peace*, 139; 10 *Rand Daily Mail*, 1 May 1976; 11 Allen, John, *Rabble Rouser for Peace*, 154; 12 Du Boulay, Shirley, *Tutu — Voice of the Voiceless*, 130; 13 Allen, John, *Rabble Rouser for Peace*, 176; 14 www.nobel.se/peace/laureates/1984/presentation-speech; 15 Du Boulay, Shirley, *Tutu — Voice of the Voiceless*, 250; 16 Allen, John, *Rabble Rouser for Peace*, 311; 17 Ibid. 370; 18 Ibid. 374.

Other quotations are from the following sources: pp. 26 (top), 28, 30, 34, 36–37, 39 (bottom), 42, 45, 49, 51, 52, 54, 57, 61, 62, 68, 69, 72–73, 75, 79, 83 (bottom), 84, 87 and 91 — Tutu, Desmond, *God Has a Dream — A Vision of Hope For Our Time*; pp. 26 (bottom), 32–33, 35, 39 (top), 40, 53, 58, 59, 65, 67 and 90 — Tutu, Naomi, *The Words of Desmond Tutu*; pp. 31, 85 and 92 — Tutu, Desmond, *No Future Without Forgiveness*; pp. 43, 46–47, 55, 81 and 88 — Tutu, Desmond and Allen, John, (ed.), *The Rainbow People of God*; pp. 77 and 83 — Tutu, Desmond, *Hope and Suffering — Sermons and Speeches*.